Downhill In-line Skating

by Nick Cook

Consultant:
Rick Babington
Vice President of Operations
USA Inline Racing

CAPSTONE BOOKS

an imprint of Capstone Press
Mankato, Minnesota

Capstone Books are published by Capstone Press
151 Good Counsel Drive, P.O. Box 669, Mankato, Minnesota 56002
http://www.capstone-press.com

Library of Congress Cataloging-in-Publication Data
Cook, Nick, 1954–
    Downhill in-line skating/by Nick Cook.
    p.cm.—(Extreme sports)
    Includes bibliographical references (p. 45) and index.
    Summary: Describes the history of in-line skating and the equipment, techniques,
skills, and safety concerns involved in this sport.
    ISBN 0-7368-0482-X
    1. In-line skating—Juvenile literature. [1. In-line skating.] I. Title. II. Series.
GV859.73.C66 2000
796.21—dc21   99-053303

Editorial Credits
Angela Kaelberer, editor; Timothy Halldin, cover designer; Kia Bielke,
    production designer; Heidi Schoof, photo researcher

Photo Credits
Dugald Bremner Studio/Dugald Bremner, 10
Jack Gescheidt, 15, 16, 20, 24, 26, 30, 36, 39
Mercury Press/Isaac Hernández, cover, 4, 9, 18, 23, 28–29, 33, 34, 43
Photo Network/Mary Messenger, 7
StreetSki, 40
Unicorn Stock/Terry Barner, 12

1 2 3 4 5 6 05 04 03 02 01 00

Table of Contents

Chapter 1
Downhill
In-line Skating

Downhill in-line skaters race down hills. These skaters wear in-line skates that look like ice skates with wheels. In-line skates have wheels attached in a straight line to the bottom of the skate boot.

In-line skating became popular in the late 1980s and early 1990s. It was one of the fastest growing sports in the United States during the 1990s.

Many athletes use in-line skates to train for other sports. Basic movements in skating are

Downhill in-line skaters race down hills.

similar to movements in other sports. For example, downhill skiing and in-line skating have almost the same moves. Downhill skiers use in-line skates to practice their sport during the summer. Some people even wear in-line skates to play sports such as hockey, basketball, or soccer.

In-line Racing

In-line skaters began competing in races in the 1980s. The first in-line racers were speed skaters. Speed skaters race on oval tracks or road courses. Oval tracks usually range from 100 to 200 meters (328 to 656 feet) in length. Road courses usually are 400 meters (1,312 feet) or longer. Road courses can be as long as 138 kilometers (86 miles).

Some speed in-line skaters performed stunts and jumps as they skated. These skaters created a new sport called aggressive in-line skating. Skaters receive points for their stunts and jumps during aggressive in-line competitions.

Downhill in-line skating combines speed skating and downhill skiing. Downhill skaters skate on paved courses on hills. These courses can be more than 1 mile (1.6 kilometers) long. Downhill skaters do not receive points for doing

The first in-line racers were speed skaters.

stunts. A downhill skater's goal is to reach the bottom of the hill in the shortest amount of time.

In-line athletes wear different types of skates because each sport has special requirements. For example, in-line hockey players make many sharp turns. In-line hockey skates have features such as wide wheels that help skaters turn sharply. Downhill skaters' skates have features that help them go faster. These features include longer frames and extra wheels. More wheels mean that less of the skater's weight is distributed to each wheel. This allows each wheel to roll faster.

Downhill Courses

Most downhill in-line racers skate on smoothly paved downhill streets. These streets are blocked to traffic during races. Skaters prefer newly paved streets. They call these streets "black ice." These courses have few holes or bumps to slow the skaters down.

Barriers line the courses. They help keep skaters on the course and spectators off the course. Spectators are people who watch races. The barriers must be soft to protect skaters who accidentally hit them. Hay bales or poles with mattresses wrapped around them often serve as barriers.

Skating Classes and Styles

Some downhill in-line skaters skate just for fun. These recreational skaters often are called citizen skaters. Other downhill skaters are professionals. They earn a living from the prize money they receive from skating in competitions. Many professional skaters

Barriers protect both downhill in-line skaters and spectators during crashes.

---

compete for teams sponsored by skate manufacturers. These companies pay for the skaters' equipment and other racing costs.

Downhill in-line skaters use strategies to race well. They plan ways to increase their speed. They select the best skates and other equipment. They also analyze each course. They figure out how they can cut seconds off their racing time. They practice on a course many times before a competition.

Chapter 2
History

Peoplo have used skates for about 3,000 years. In about 1000 B.C., hunters in what is now northern Europe used the first skates. These hunters fastened animal bones to the soles of their shoes. The bones helped them chase animals across ice. By the 1200s, people replaced the bones with wooden blades. In the late 1500s, people used skates with metal blades to move across ice.

Roller Skates
Roller skates were invented much later than ice skates. In 1760, a Belgian man named Joseph Merlin wanted to impress people at a party. He

In-line skating traces its history back nearly 3,000 years.

Roller skates have two sets of wheels.

attached wooden spools to his shoes and skated into the party. But the spools did not allow him to stop or turn. He was injured when he crashed into a mirror.

A French inventor named M. Peitibled created in-line skates in 1819. His first skates had two to four metal wheels in a straight line. These wheels were not flexible. They did not move easily. This made the skates difficult to steer.

In 1863, James Plimpton invented the modern roller skate. This skate had four wheels. Plimpton put a pair of wheels under the shoe's toe. Another pair of wheels went under the heel. Rubber pads on the wheels helped the wheels turn easily.

Modern In-line Skates

In the 1960s, the Chicago Roller Skate Company manufactured an in-line boot skate. At that time, few roller skaters were interested in using this new type of skate.

In 1979, a Minnesota hockey player named Scott Olson was in a sporting goods store. He found an old in-line skate. Olson and his brother Brennan improved the skates. They added rubber heel brakes and wheels made of polyurethane. This hard, rubber-like plastic is very strong.

Scott Olson bought the Chicago Roller Skate Company's patents for in-line skates. In 1981, Olson created the Rollerblade brand of in-line skates. These skates had a row of four wheels. Metal rods called axles secured the wheels to a metal frame. This frame was attached to the center of the boot.

Hockey players were Rollerblade Inc.'s first customers. These athletes used these skates to train during the summer. Soon, other people began using in-line skates for fun and exercise. Other skate companies soon began to make in-line skates.

In-line Races

By 1989, many roller speed skaters had switched to in-line skates. The Fédération Internationale de Roller Skating (FIRS) governs roller-skating sports around the world. In 1991, FIRS allowed in-line skaters to compete in roller speed skating events.

In 1991, athletes and skate manufacturers joined to form the International Inline Skating Association (IISA). This organization sets rules for in-line safety and trains people to teach in-line skating.

Several skaters' organizations sponsor in-line road races. These organizations include

Many roller speed skaters switched to in-line skates by the late 1980s.

USA Inline Racing (USAIR), USA Roller Skating, and the Canadian In-line and Roller-Skating Association (CIRSA). In-line road races take place on flat, paved surfaces. Athletes who skate in these road races receive points. These points depend on how high skaters place in the races. These points often determine which skaters move on to international competitions such as the International Roller Contest.

The Beginning of Downhill In-line Skating

The ESPN television network invented downhill in-line skating. ESPN sponsors a competition each year called the X-Games. Athletes compete in different extreme sports at these games. Downhill in-line skating first appeared in the 1995 X-Games. Only men skated in the downhill in-line event the first year. In 1996, ESPN added a women's division.

In 1999, ESPN removed downhill in-line skating from the X-Games. Not enough viewers watched the competition. But downhill in-line skaters can compete in other races. These include the Mammoth Downhill Skate Festival, the International Roller Contest, and Westwood Ski and Sports Club events.

Downhill in-line races were part of the X-Games from 1995 to 1999.

Chapter 3
Equipment and Safety

Downhill in-line skaters' equipment is designed for speed. It must be lightweight. Heavy equipment can slow down a skater. Downhill skaters' equipment also must be aerodynamic. This equipment is designed to let air flow over it easily. This helps skaters reach greater speeds.

Downhill skating can be dangerous. Some downhill skaters reach speeds of more than 60 miles (97 kilometers) per hour. These skaters may crash into course barriers or each other. Downhill skaters must wear gear to protect themselves during falls or crashes.

Downhill skaters' equipment must be aerodynamic.

Downhill in-line skaters wear skates with five or six wheels.

Boots, Liners, and Frames

In-line skate boots are made from leather and fiberglass or carbon fiber. These materials are strong and lightweight. Downhill skaters need boots that fit well. Top-quality boots can be molded to the skater's feet. Skaters use a heat gun to mold their boots to their feet. Molded boots keep the shape of the skater's foot after they are removed.

The inner part of the boot that covers the foot is called the liner. Liners provide comfort and support for the foot. Liners are made of foam. The thickness of a liner is called its density. Liners with high densities are hard and stiff. Those with low densities are soft and flexible. Most downhill in-line skaters wear boots with high-density liners. These liners keep the foot from moving around in the boot. This gives the skater greater control.

Skate frames fasten to the boot. The frames hold the skate's wheels. The frames are made of aluminum. This metal is lightweight and strong. Aluminum frames absorb shock from rough courses. Downhill skaters have skate frames that are longer and stiffer than aggressive in-line skaters' frames. The long, stiff frames give skaters more control at high speeds.

Wheels

Downhill in-line skates have five or six wheels. Recreational in-line skates have four wheels. The extra wheels allow downhill skaters to skate at higher speeds. Downhill skates are longer to fit the extra wheels. They are 12.8 to 16 inches (33 to 41 centimeters) long.

Wheels vary in size, durometer, and footprint. Durometer is the measure of a wheel's hardness and durability. Footprint is the thickness of a wheel.

Wheel sizes are measured in millimeters. Sizes range from 44 to 82 millimeters (1.7 to 3.2 inches). The most common size is 72 millimeters (2.8 inches). Downhill skaters usually use larger wheels. Larger wheels are faster than smaller ones. This is because they travel a greater distance each time they roll. Downhill skate wheels usually are 80 millimeters (3.1 inches).

The "A" scale measures the durometer of skate wheels. On this scale, the softest wheels rate 1A and the hardest wheels rate 100A. Wheels with low durometer absorb bumps well. But they wear out faster than wheels with higher durometer. Wheels with higher durometer also roll faster on black ice.

Skaters choose wheels to match their skating style. Skaters want the right mix of a smooth ride and durable wheels. Recreational skates usually have 78A durometer wheels. Downhill skaters may combine 78A and 82A wheels. They put the

Downhill skaters usually wear skates with large wheels.

softer 78A wheels near the skate's front to smooth out the ride. They put the harder 82A wheels near the skate's back for speed.

Footprint is measured in millimeters. The standard skate wheel is 24 millimeters (.95 inches) thick. Wheels with a larger footprint have greater traction and stability. A downhill skater needs a thinner footprint for speed. Racing wheels are thinner at the edge than the middle. Only the thin part of the wheel hits the pavement. This reduces

A helmet is a downhill in-line skater's most important piece of safety equipment.

friction between the wheel and the street. Friction is the force produced when two objects rub against each other. Friction slows down skaters.

Bearings

Each wheel has two sets of bearings. These small metal balls are located between the axle and the wheel. Bearings help wheels turn smoothly. They also reduce friction by allowing the wheel to roll around the axle.

The Annular Bearing Engineering Council (ABEC) rates bearings. This organization rates bearings using odd numbers from 1 to 9 according to the bearing's tolerance. This term refers to how tightly the bearing is packed within the axle. Tightly-packed bearings usually produce less friction and allow the skater to race faster. Most recreational in-line skates have ABEC 1- or 3-rated bearings. Racing skates may use ABEC 5- or 7-rated bearings.

Helmets

A helmet is a downhill in-line skater's most important piece of safety gear. Helmets help protect skaters from head injuries if they fall or crash.

Helmets have tough plastic or fiberglass shells with foam liners. Skaters adjust their helmets to make sure the helmets fit their heads snugly. A good helmet is both lightweight and strong.

Padding and Body Suits

Downhill in-line skaters must wear protective gear to guard against muscle and bone injuries.

Downhill skaters wear protective gear.

Some of this gear also protects skaters from
a painful burn called "road rash." Road rash
occurs when a skater's bare skin scrapes
against the road.

Skaters wear padding. Knee, wrist, and
elbow pads reduce scrapes and bruises. They
also help protect skaters from breaking bones
or suffering muscle injuries.

Wrist guards protect skaters' hands and wrists. People usually extend their arms forward when they fall. Skaters may hit the pavement hard with their palms open. The shock may cause wrist and hand bones to break. Wrist guards hold wrists firmly between stiff plastic or metal plates.

Knee and elbow guards have hard plastic over fabric pads. The guards protect the knees and elbows during falls. The high speeds of downhill skating cause skaters to slide during a fall. The pads must not move when a skater skids over the street.

Some skaters also wear hockey gloves. These gloves contain a great deal of padding. This prevents injury to wrists, hands, and thumbs during falls.

Most downhill in-line skaters also wear body suits. Some of these suits are made of leather. Others are made from synthetic materials such as Lycra spandex. This manufactured material is lightweight and fits tightly. The tight fit helps skaters be more aerodynamic. Lycra spandex also is cooler than leather.

Helmet

Gloves

Pads

Boot

544

Body Suit

Frame

Axle

Wheels

Chapter 4
Skills

Downhill in-line skaters use a number of skills and abilities. These include balance, endurance, and mental strategy.

Training
Downhill in-line skaters develop their skills through training. Skaters mainly race during the summer months. But they train throughout the year.

Downhill skaters warm up before each training period. They begin by skating slowly and smoothly for at least five minutes. They gradually increase their speed. This allows their heart and muscles to work more efficiently.

Downhill in-line skaters use a number of skills and abilities.

Skaters then work out by skating at speeds ranging from 15 to 25 miles (24 to 40 kilometers) per hour. They skate for about 30 minutes. They increase this time with each workout. This helps them build their endurance.

Skaters stretch after each workout. This helps prevent skaters' muscles from becoming tight. Tight muscles are easily injured. Skaters mainly concentrate on the legs, lower back, and stomach area as they stretch.

Skaters also train with weights. Skaters lift weights to build their muscles and endurance.

Racing Moves

Downhill in-line skaters must think about aerodynamics as they skate. They perform some special moves in order to reduce drag. This force is created when air strikes a moving object. Drag slows down the object.

Skaters reduce drag by performing a tuck. They crouch low over their skates and hold their arms against their sides or in front of their bodies. Skaters have less air resistance in this position.

Downhill in-line skaters tuck and draft to reduce drag.

Skaters also draft to reduce drag. Skaters draft by skating very close behind another skater. This creates less air resistance around the second skater. The second skater then can maintain speed while using less energy. Skaters sometimes take turns being the lead skater.

Strategy

Skaters also use mental strategies as they race. They plan each race. They think about the best ways to move around other skaters or down the hill.

In the first downhill races, skaters skated as fast as they could throughout the race. A fast start and a good tuck allowed skaters to win races without drafting.

Later, downhill skaters began to skate differently during races. Today, skaters start slower. They stay in a pack and draft each other for the first quarter of the race. Finally, one skater "jumps." This sudden burst of speed starts a sprint toward the finish line.

Skaters sometimes finish the race with an "eagle hawk." This happens when two skaters are very close to each other at the finish line. The skaters stretch one leg forward as far as possible to get their skate across the finish line first. The skater with the first skate to cross the finish line wins the race.

One skater usually "jumps" at the end of a race.

Chapter 5
Competition

The X-Games officials' decision to drop downhill in-line skating hurt the sport. But professional and citizen skaters can compete in a number of other racing events.

Downhill In-line Races
The longest downhill in-line race in the United States is the Mammoth Downhill Skate Festival. This race takes place each September on Mammoth Mountain near the city of Mammoth Lakes, California. Professional skaters compete on a steep, 1.3-mile (2-kilometer) course during the three-day

Downhill in-line skaters can compete in a number of racing events.

event. Citizen skaters race on a more level 1-mile (1.6-kilometer) course. Professional skaters average speeds of more than 50 miles (80 kilometers) per hour.

The International Roller Contest is one of the largest in-line skating competitions. This three-day competition takes place each August in Lausanne, Switzerland. Skaters can compete in aggressive, downhill, and speed contests. The downhill course twists through the city's streets. It takes skaters about three minutes to skate the 3-kilometer (1.9-mile) downhill course. Skaters average speeds of 37 miles (60 kilometers) per hour. Some reach speeds of 54 miles (87 kilometers) per hour.

The Westwood Ski and Sports Club of California holds regular practice sessions and competitions in Los Angeles. These competitions include many ski-style events. These include downhill as well as slalom events. Slalom events are similar to alpine skiing. Slalom skaters race downhill on courses marked by plastic cones or hinged gates. Skaters must race around each cone or through each swinging gate.

Professional downhill in-line skaters earn prize money when they win races.

Professional Skaters

Professional downhill in-line skaters earn prize money when they win races. But the prize money often does not pay for all the costs of professional racing. These costs include race fees, travel expenses, and equipment costs.

Most professional downhill in-line skaters have sponsors. These companies or organizations help skaters pay for entry fees, travel costs, and

equipment. In return, skaters use the companies' equipment or products during races. Some skaters promote the companies' equipment or products in TV commercials and magazine advertisements. Most major in-line skate manufacturers sponsor a team of professional skaters.

New Developments
Downhill in-line skating has had several changes during recent years. Skaters have developed new variations of the sport. These include downhill skating and off-road downhill skating.

Downhill skating uses skates that are longer versions of downhill in-line skates. They look similar to downhill skis. People also call this sport downhill in-line skiing. In 1996, skater David Lucht formed Alternative International Sports (AIS) to govern this sport. Lucht's brother Doug also is a downhill skater. In March 1998, Doug Lucht set a downhill speed record of 63 miles (101 kilometers) per hour.

In September 1998, AIS held a downhill competition in Fountain Hills, Arizona. Each

In March 1998, Doug Lucht set a downhill skating speed record of 63 miles (101 kilometers) per hour.

skater completed the course three times. The top 10 skaters earned an additional run. Skaters Jeff Hamilton and Graham Wilkie won the event. They each broke Lucht's record with a time of 64 miles (103 kilometers) per hour. Downhill skate races also are part of the Mammoth Downhill Skate Festival and the Australian Extreme Games.

The newest type of downhill in-line skating is off-road downhill. These skaters skate down unpaved, sloping trails. They wear skates with large, knobby wheels. These wheels have bumps that help them grip the unpaved trails. The wheels look similar to tiny mountain bike wheels.

BladeCross is an off-road skating competition sponsored by Rollerblade Inc. This competition includes cross country, downhill, and slalom events. These events are held in several locations in the United States each year.

Off-road downhill skaters skate down unpaved, sloping trails.

Words To Know

aerodynamics (air-oh-dye-NAM-iks)—the science that deals with the motion of air

axle (AK-suhl)—a rod in the center of a wheel; the wheel turns around the axle.

bearing (BAIR-ing)—a small, round metal part of a wheel; bearings help reduce friction.

draft (DRAFT)—to skate closely behind another skater; skaters draft in order to reduce drag.

drag (DRAG)—the force created when air strikes a moving object; drag slows the object.

durometer (duh-ROM-uh-tur)—a unit that measures a skate wheel's hardness and durability

frame (FRAYM)—the in-line skate part that connects the wheels to the boot

friction (FRIK-shuhn)—the force produced when two objects rub against each other

polyurethane (pah-lee-YUR-uh-thayn)—a hard, rubber-like plastic used to make skate wheels

To Learn More

Chalmers, Aldie. *The Fantastic Book of In-Line Skating.* Brookfield, Conn.: Copper Beech Books, 1997.

Edwards, Chris. *The Young Inline Skater.* New York: DK Publishing, 1996.

McKenna, Anne T. *Aggressive In-Line Skating.* Extreme Sports. Mankato, Minn.: Capstone Books, 1999.

Savage, Jeff. *In-Line Skating Basics.* New Action Sports. Mankato, Minn.: Capstone Books, 1996.

Useful Addresses

Canadian In-Line and Roller Skating Association (CIRSA)
679 Queens Quay West, Unit 117
Toronto, ON M5V 3A9
Canada

International Inline Skating Association (IISA)
201 North Front Street
Suite 306
Wilmington, NC 28401

USA Inline Racing (USAIR)
1271 Boynton Street, #15
Glendale, CA 91205

Westwood Ski and Sports Club
P.O. Box 24534
Los Angeles, CA 90024

Internet Sites

International Inline Skating Association (IISA)
http://www.iisa.org

N2inline.com
http://www.n2inline.com

Skate FAQs (Frequently Asked Questions)
http://www.skatefaq.com

USA Inline Racing (USAIR)
http://www.usainlineracing.com

Westwood Ski & Sports Club
http://members.aol.com/wwskiclub/inline.htm

Index